Coping with
Temper
Tantrums

Also available in the NANNY KNOWS BEST series
Successful Potty Training
Easy Weaning & First Feeding
Stop Your Baby's Crying

Coping with
Temper
Tantrums

Nanny Smith

with Nina Grunfeld

This edition published in 1996 by Limited Editions

First published in the United Kingdom in 1996
by Vermilion, an imprint of Ebury Press,
Random House, 20 Vauxhall Bridge Road,
London SW1V 2SA

Random House Australia (Pty) Limited
20 Alfred Street, Milsons Point, Sydney
New South Wales 2061, Australia

Random House New Zealand Limited
18 Poland Road, Glenfield
Auckland 10, New Zealand

Random House South Africa (Pty) Limited
PO Box 337, Bergvlei, South Africa

Random House UK Limited Reg. No. 954009

A CIP catalogue record for this book is available from the
British Library.

Printed and bound in Great Britain by
Mackays of Chatham PLC, Chatham, Kent

CONTENTS

AUTHOR'S NOTE

Unless a specific child is being written about, throughout the book your baby is referred to as 'he', not because of any bias but to differentiate you, the mother or child carer, from your baby.

CHAPTER ONE

What are Tantrums?

APROLONGED TANTRUM IN A CHILD CAN WORRY, almost frighten, parents, especially when the child is a little bit older because it is alarming and the parent doesn't know what to do. I remember once watching Hitler on television and he was shouting and raging: I looked at him and thought he looked as if he were having a tantrum – his arm was up in the air and he was almost stamping his foot and shouting and shouting. In a way I suppose he was having a 'controlled' tantrum. Watching a child's tantrum can be very disturbing for an adult and I remember thinking that Hitler's use of 'tantrums' – for effect – was part of the way he must have frightened many adults into submission.

Adults are frightened of tantrums
Most adults are embarrassed about children having tantrums, making excuses for them and sometimes

slapping, shaking, and shouting at them. They are so angry with the child for having a tantrum that in their frustration they sometimes have a sort of adult tantrum. Of course people on the whole have an idealised idea of childhood and if the child has always played happily with his toys and eaten all his lunch and then he suddenly turns agin everything, then adults do get very worried and cross. And yet in a funny sort of way it is often the adult who has the tantrum first. When an adult says, 'Don't do that,' to the child and the child then does it and the adult gets very angry and spanks the child, then the adult is having the tantrum – not the child.

Most children have tantrums

One can say tantrums can happen at any age: we think of a child shouting and screaming, pushing people away and falling on to the floor and drumming his heels – that's a sort of classic tantrum, but adults getting very angry and saying things they shouldn't are having tantrums too, in a way. A baby lying in a cot having his meals on time has no need for tantrums, but once he becomes upright and on his feet he can only express his unhappiness by tantrums. So if a child is going to have tantrums, then most children start at around two-ish, which is why we say the 'terrible twos'. Of course there are babies who start having tantrums at a year old and may carry on having them until they are four or five and going to school. Some older children do get very angry too and sometimes a child who has never had tantrums around the ages of two and three, because of changing circumstances – such as his parents' divorce – may begin having terrible angry fits at any age, as a result of insecurity. Insecurity brings sensitivity and with it both understanding and therefore anger. In one form or another a sensitive person can have tantrums for a lifetime because I don't think there ever really is a time when one stops minding about things. When you get older you can see all sorts of different ways of looking at things and you can find ways of controlling and channelling your anger, but when you are very young and angry, which is often caused by a disappointment, you have a tantrum.

Very occasionally you will meet a child who doesn't ever have tantrums, but there aren't very many of them. Almost all children go through a period of having tantrums – some more excessive than others. The great thing is to ease them through the tantrum stage by not dwelling on it, so it is not always in the back of the child's mind.

When is a tantrum likely to happen?

As an adult you can quite often anticipate that one of your 'tantrums' might occur. The day starts badly with a lot of frustrating things happening and you swallow hard and count to ten. Then yet more frustrating things happen: the telephone call or letter you are waiting for doesn't arrive, the greengrocer hasn't got the one thing you needed and so on. Then finally something happens, usually when you are with someone you really care for, but not always, and it is the final straw that breaks the camel's back – and you snap and say things you regret, just like a 'tantrum'. It's spontaneous, you can't help what you are doing or saying. It all happens so quickly. Of course as an adult you can work out why you snapped, but with a child you are not always aware of why he is having a tantrum, you can only guess at it.

Yet sometimes you can have a really frustrating day and yet you can cope with it and feel all right so I think tantrums are to do with more than just the frustration of the moment and are symptomatic of other things that one is feeling. The same goes for children too. Tantrums very often seem to occur in adults when they are tired, hungry, depressed, premenstrual or hung over, and it's the same with children – except with different causes. You may even find your child has his tantrums on your 'bad' days. It's almost as if he is mirroring your mood.

You often see children having tantrums in the street which one can see are often the result of the child being over-tired. Just as with adults when one is over-tired it is difficult to cope with life, so it is with children too. It may be that the child has been on a long walk and has depleted resources. It may also be that he is hungry and it is getting on for eating time. Certainly when collect-ing children from school they are often bad-tempered but once they have eaten they are quite amenable and happy. We also always used to reckon that the second half of a party, after the children have had tea, went much better than the first. When you arrive at a party with children, at first some never want to join in and others are a bit aggressive, but once they have had the tea they all join in quite happily – rather like putting petrol in the car. I think very often when children have tantrums it's because they are hungry.

Why a tantrum?

Some children do have a very short fuse and the slightest thing causes them to roll about on the floor kicking and screaming. The tantrum is a safety valve, a way of releasing anger so that it doesn't build up inside and the child gets more and more depressed and muddled. Although the child may regret it, having the tantrum is his way of releasing tension.

Children have tantrums when they are frustrated in some way – either by something they can't do, like build a tall tower or undo their coat toggles – or by your not wanting them to do something or interfering with their plans in one way or another (see Commands To Avoid, page 42). So by having the tantrum, whether it is large or small, they are channelling their aggression against themselves, and often against you. Instead of hitting out at you they have a tantrum and although they haven't consciously thought, Shall I have a tantrum now or not? The tantrum has happened spontaneously. Once over, the frustration has gone.

What forms do tantrums take?

Tan-trum is a funny word. It describes what's happening, the drumming, the feeling of frustration.

A good old-fashioned tantrum is when a child flings himself on the floor, screaming and flailing his arms and legs about, but there are many different forms. Some children stamp their feet and hurl things, others are so very angry they dash about, running round the room screaming. With younger children, screaming is the one thing that dominates the tantrum and I've heard of children screaming until they make themselves sick or holding their breath until they lose consciousness. When children are older they sulk which is a silent sort of tantrum.

Stopping a tantrum

I think it is almost impossible to stop a tantrum happening, but it depends on what the frustration might be about. If a child is furious and you can see a tantrum is about to happen you can say, 'Can I just ask you something?' or 'Come on, let's put your coat on, we're going to the shops.' Distracting them is the best course but never get angry about the impending tantrum, just keep things on a light note. If, no matter what you do or say, they keep on, I would just let them explode – they are angry and they want everyone to know it. I certainly would never comment on it, nor try to stop them.

Sometimes you'll find that older siblings start imitating the baby as he is about to start having tantrums, making fun of him, which can lighten the situation and so avert the tantrum. That's children sorting it out, in their world, but I would never do the same thing; that's adults trying to be like children.

What is really wrong?

Occasionally you can work out why your child is having a tantrum and can see the reason for his frustration, but very often you cannot imagine why it is happening or why so frequently. But you should always look for the reason because there will always be one. He is being frustrated for one reason or another, and the first thing you must do is look to yourself, because maybe as the child is daily getting older you are changing in your outlook towards him, possibly being a little firmer or expecting a little more of him. It may be that you're having another baby and so are tired and more irritable, or it may be just before your period, or perhaps you've got extra demands made on you at home or work and are feeling generally tense and more snappy than usual. All these things can affect your child.

You may also have to contend with criticism from your husband, your mother, friends and other well-meaning people who might have been saying to you about your child, 'Oh, he's twenty-four months, he ought to be able to do that,' but you must ignore them. People put children mentally in little boxes and tend to expect them to do things and then get cross when they can't. They forget that children should be allowed to develop at their own pace – a child with a strong will is going to resent being put into a box instead of being allowed to feel his own way. People so often say to children, 'You can't do that – you're not a baby any more,' but they are babies for quite a long time. You must go along with the child, try to get under his skin and stick up for him as his own person, try to see things through his eyes. I always used to say in a child's hearing, 'I think Sarah is wonderful.' For a child to hear this is much kinder and more helpful than overhearing, 'I think Sarah is so cruel.' Help your child have a feeling of self-worth (see also Chapter Two).

CHAPTER TWO

Four Golden Rules

M Y FOUR GOLDEN RULES WON'T NECESSARILY
transform a child who is prone to tantrums
into a trouble-free child, but if you try to
follow them they might help you both to enjoy these
first few years of childhood, helping you to understand
the reasons for the tantrums, which might result in a
happier child – and a happier parent. With luck, they
might even stop the tantrums. Most importantly, they
might help ensure that your child grows up in a happy,
loving and understanding environment.

The first golden rule seems so obvious that it
shouldn't need to be mentioned.

The first Golden Rule

✦ Listen to your child
(Whether he's talking to you or himself)

One of my pet hates is a child saying, 'What's that, Mum?' and the mother ignores him. The child says it about four or five times and the mother could so easily answer, 'I don't know,' or briefly tell him what it is – 'Oh, it's a thing you put tea in,' or whatever – but she ignores her child. It is terribly rude and so easy to avoid. Even if you are very busy, all you have to say is, 'I don't know,' and then at least you have answered him. A bright child will get very angry if he doesn't get an answer.

It only takes a minute
Quite often children ask, 'What's that?' just for something to say. They can see it's a hat and don't really want to know but they do go through a stage of saying 'What's that?' and 'Why?' for no good reason. It is annoying but it is just a phase and I have been known to answer 'Why not?' simply because the habit has been going on for so long. I wouldn't say it initially but only once they have asked a lot of questions. A child won't stamp his feet and say, 'Tell me! Tell me!' because he doesn't really want to know. Of course, as soon as children are a little older they really do want to know the answers to their questions.

Ignoring a child is unkind and initially makes him so

frustrated that it can bring on a tantrum, but in the end you will find that a neglected child doesn't bother to ask questions because he knows he is not going to get an answer and his senses have been dulled.

If children ask for help, listen

Very often adults do expect a lot from children, especially the very young. I have often watched girls of three after ballet class being told by their keepers, 'Put your shoes on!', 'Get your clothes on!' and they were so worn out by their ballet class and so worn down by their keepers that they didn't have tantrums.

There was also a lot of, 'You've put it on the wrong foot, you silly thing,' which must slowly reduce the child's confidence and may make a sensitive child withdraw. In the end the child won't bother to ask for help because he knows he is supposed to do it himself. He'll feel insecure and it may bring out a certain aggression in him: he is receiving aggression and so he too will become aggressive – a shover and a pusher.

You can recognise an unhappy child

If you continually criticise a child you take away all his confidence and if you shout at him too often then eventually it dulls his senses. I remember children coming for tea and it was so easy to tell the children who had been appreciated at home and cared for and those who had been told off and ignored. A child who is appreciated is a child who is alert, interesting, has good manners, is able to talk about things, however small, knows how to play and is interested in whatever toys you have. He would just fit in. A child who is neglected at home is unable to settle, and wanders around the house opening drawers and cupboards. He can't stay in the one place, nor can he really play. He is often prone to exaggeration, saying things that you know can't be true, such as, 'We're going to go to Spain for the weekend.' It is very sad. No one in his household has really cared for him.

When children play they copy

Listen to your child all through the day and by the child's way of speaking, attitude, and so on, you can tell if all is well or if there is something worrying him. I remember visiting a little girl once and when I admired her doll, she snatched it from me and hurled it across the room and said, 'She's a naughty little girl.' It was something that had happened to her – at some stage she too had been treated like that.

You may be a very busy person and you don't realise that sometimes you criticise your child and are negative and rude about him, but if you listen to your child you will hear him do the same to himself or to a doll, or just saying, 'Naughty boy,' to himself and slapping his own wrists. Alas, it may not be you whose behaviour he is copying, it might be a keeper who is there sometimes for a day and your child may be copying what has happened to him on that day. So watch out for warning signs because children are transparent, and copy everything they see around them. This is sometimes how you can work out the cause of a specific unhappiness. By listening to your child you can hear what's worrying him.

You can hear if a child is sad

You don't really need to ask children if or why they are unhappy: you can observe the patterns of their day, the remarks they make, the things they say when they are playing and drawing. Because you know your own child you can tell if something isn't quite right – you know there is something up by the way he behaves, the way he answers your questions. When he gets a little older you can tell when something is up at school. If he is quiet and suddenly doesn't want to go to school you can tell he is having a problem – unless he is about to fall ill and is feeling low.

Listening to children is very rewarding. When you tuck them up to go to sleep they might say something that indicates they have a fear of some kind, and they try to keep you longer and longer to say goodnight. So, without dwelling on it, when you leave them I would just leave the door wide open so they know you are there, or say you're going to make the supper for ten minutes and you'll be back – and go back – and then they have the reassurance that you are there. If you sleep easily it is because you have had a happy day. If the child has a very secure life during the day then he will sleep peacefully.

When children play they talk

A mother once told me that she couldn't be doing with all the mess her child made at home when he was painting: 'Anyway, he can do it at playschool.' I thought this was an extraordinary thing to say as you can protect furniture and carpets perfectly easily. I also felt it was rather sad that he was not allowed to paint at home, but had to wait until the days he went to playschool. It is very good for a child to have a variety of interests at home and painting is such fun – I have never met a child who did not enjoy painting – dipping the brush into the pot of paint and putting it all over the paper, and it does speak volumes. An exuberant child and a child who has a worry will paint in a different manner and you'll soon learn when something is troubling him and you are helping him to express it. Playing with playdough or Plasticine or singing loudly or running in the park are all ways of helping the child to release his anxieties and helping you to find out about them. Or on a rainy day you could say to the child, 'Let's draw some pictures – what shall we draw?' I remember once saying to a little girl I knew, 'Shall I draw a picture? I know, I'll draw you.' She then suggested I drew Mummy and Daddy and her elder brother, so I asked if I should draw her brand-new baby sister and she said, 'Yes, draw her – put her in Mummy's tummy.'

Listen to your child and he'll listen to you

So many people say, 'My child doesn't listen to me,' but

if all they have been doing is telling the child what to do and what not to do then children do rebel. Up to the age of five all children are rebellious and want to do the opposite of what is suggested. It therefore seems to me that it must be better if you can avoid telling the child what to do and what not to do as much as possible (see The second Golden Rule, page 23). Instead of continually giving the child commands you must allow him to get on with his day. What he needs is a friend who guides him but a friend who is also fun.

I was once contacted by parents with a three-year-old daughter who had been 'difficult' since the age of one and now regularly had screaming tantrums where she was inconsolable and physically scratched her own face in anger and frustration. Her parents told me they had tried offering love, being firm and sometimes even being very angry. When they got in touch with me their daughter had recently developed a stammer which came and went in tune with her moods. Her mother said she was bossy with other children and refused to share her toys.

I felt very sorry for this little girl. Her parents had tried to mould her and, when she had fought against that, instead of listening to her and going along with her whenever they could, they had been angry. I told them that from now on they had to give their daughter a peaceful life,

that she was a person in her own right and
should be accepted as such and not always made
to do certain things and forbidden to do others
simply to conform to their pattern. If she was
bossy with other children it was because they
have been bossy to her. Of course, they were
doing what they thought they ought to but, like
them, their daughter was very strong-minded and
so they would have to pay a little more attention
to her wishes and feelings and try to see things
from her point of view. They shouldn't, for
example, make her share her toys – this would
happen naturally in a few years' time if they set
her a good example. The best way for a child to
learn is if you teach by example.

Scratching her face during a tantrum did
seem an extreme form of registering her anger,
and showed that she must have been at the end
of her tether. I suggested that once they had
taken a very much softer line in dealing with her
and stopped giving orders and started being a
chum to her, she would probably soon stop
scratching herself and stop stuttering as well,
although she would not stop having tantrums
altogether for a while. I told the parents to try to
build her up rather than put her down. I also told
them to make sure that they never talked about
the stammering or the tantrums or the face
scratching in front of anyone when their daughter

was in earshot, or the problems might become more extreme.

A problem of any kind should never be spoken about in the child's hearing, as they understand from a very early age what you are talking about.

The second Golden Rule

✦ Home is not the army
(Children should not have to obey commands)

I always aim not to give commands because a small child's life should be the same more or less every day so there really is no need to be telling the child to do and not to do things. People are busy and so of course some people will shout, 'Come on! Hurry up!' and one wouldn't denigrate them but my aim is always for a peaceful life.

Lead with routine, not commands
If a small child's life is more or less routine-led then if lunch is ready there is no need to say, 'Come and have lunch. Stop playing and come now!' Instead, if we have lunch at the same time every day and every day he sees me laying the table and putting the lunch out then most children climb into their chair – or try to – because food has arrived and they have eaten nothing since breakfast and are hungry. If, for example, you would rather your

child had cleaner paws, instead of saying, 'Wash your hands!' I just get a flannel and wash them while he is at the table without talking about it or, if he hasn't yet sat down, I go to the bathroom to wash my hands and take him along with me so I can wash his. This is a simple routine that happens every day and as the child gets older he will soon automatically go to the bathroom and wash his hands before lunch because it is all part of the routine. (See My Tried and Tested Routines, Chapter Six.)

What if he doesn't come and eat?

Sometimes a child does just carry on playing. He is almost stating that he is going to do what he wants to do, so I just serve him and myself and start eating; sooner or later he comes along and I wouldn't comment on it. I always feel that it was very good because the child has then made his own decision to join me at table. He's not being pushed about. As a grown-up you'd take your time, so why not as a child? If I had finished my meal and was starting to clear up before he came, then I still wouldn't tell him off but just put him in his chair and give him his meal.

Of course, if we are in a hurry then I have to say, 'Come on, let's put on your bib and get into the high chair because we promised to meet Granny and we have got to be quick,' and an intelligent child will take that in. If he gets angry then I just leave him and get him ready to go to Granny's. If he is hungry later, I do not give him a snack – he has to wait until tea-time. Sometimes children are almost testing you, as if they are thinking, Suppose I refuse to come, I wonder what she'll do. So if you say, 'We really must go now or we'll miss the bus,' and pick him up and put him in the chair, then you're chums and you can eat together. If the child really doesn't want to eat the food then I would take it away, but certainly not get angry. Sometimes he might not want to eat then regret it and want it back, which I would do. After all, we're all allowed to change our minds.

Make each part of the day a treat

I always aim to make every day happy, with funny little conversations or giving children things to play with that they enjoy, like biscuits and water for teddy's tea party. If it was a rainy day and we couldn't go out we would have lots of stories and conversations. I always go along with their dreams and fantasies – join in with them because they are fleeting and they give so much joy to the child. If the child says, 'When I grow up I am going to drive a train,' then I reply, 'Oh yes. May I come in the cab with you?' Up to a certain age children think that you are the same age as them and want you to join in their fantasies. Do so, for soon enough they won't want you to have anything to do with what they are doing.

I try to make each day relaxed, with simple pleasures so the child feels comfortable about his life without being able to put it into words. For instance bath-time is always a happy, fun time. It is always at the same time, 6 p.m., when I run the bath and the children run into the bathroom with me. I don't make it 'the end of the day' but just an extension of it and I never hurry baths. They play in the bath and then when it's time to get out – after about fifteen minutes – I help them jump out, wrap them in a large towel, cuddle and dry them. Then once they are in bed I read them a story. I never close the curtains because I feel the child might find it strange to be with people all day long and then to be shut in a room with the curtains and the door closed. So I leave the curtains open to make them feel less shut off. Obviously, if it is a very hot summer I pull the curtains across to shield the child from the hot sun, but otherwise I leave them open. I always say, 'Goodnight, sleep tight,' and come out and close the door behind me. I never ask, 'Shall I leave the door open?' but if the child asks to have it left open (which at a certain age almost all children do) then I do so, so that they can hear the sounds of the day – they are then still part of the household.

Routine avoids confrontation

There are millions of things that children don't want to do that you as their keeper are making them do and that is very frustrating. Because I keep every day more or less the same I avoid continually telling the children what to do. I also never give them a choice of doing it or not. Very often when children are offered a choice –

such as 'Would you like to put your coat on?' – it's not a choice at all, simply a chance to say 'No!' which you are then going to ignore because you have to do it anyway. The child feels that he has been asked to make a decision and you have ignored his answer and that is cause for frustration. If you have always just put his coat on without talking about it then that is accepted. Whether he wants his coat on or not it has to go on because he is going out with you – so don't ask him. Of course, if he makes a bit of a fuss which he may sometimes do, give him something else to think about to distract him from the coat being put on. It is much better to say 'I thought we might feed the ducks later, so let's put on your coat and go to the shops so we'll have time', rather than 'Put on your coat' or even 'Let's put on your coat'.

I hear so many people ask their children what they would like. The other day I heard a mother ask her three-year-old son, 'What would you like?' as they were entering the supermarket. His nose would hardly go over the counter and yet he's expected to menu plan. You know what is good for your child and you know what he likes and it is so much easier all round if you make the decisions.

Avoid commands
Within the bounds of safety you must give your child plenty of rope so he can explore and do as he wishes. You must make sure it is quite safe for him to do so. For

example, children often want to walk along walls which are rather too high for your happiness but if you hold one of his hands he can walk quite safely along the wall, so I would always rather do that than making him get down so he can't fall.

I always aim to have a situation whereby I don't have to say 'No' or 'Stop' or 'Come back'. For instance, when I am out with a child who is walking I always use reins so that the child walks beside me or a little behind or a little in front because the reins give a lot of leeway. Quite a lot of people are very anti-reins, which I find extraordinary: the child is safe and is not being grabbed or shouted at all the time. My children just used to wait at the door until their reins were put on – if they've always had them then they won't mind. Of course you can hold a child's hand when crossing the road but that gives them a tired arm holding it up for you and means that both of you have one hand occupied that could be doing other things. With reins both your hands are free. I've seen mothers wearing those straps which go from wrist to wrist and running for buses and pulling their children over so they have fallen. With reins you can prevent children falling and would never pull them over.

I also always have a nursery that is totally childproof, but even if you don't have a whole room I would aim to have a corner of a room which can be fastened off where the child can play. Otherwise you will have to make your kitchen or sitting room childproof. Any room the children are in regularly has to be more or less childproof because they are very adventurous and you don't want to keep shouting at them to 'Stay here,' 'Don't touch,' or whatever.

I once received a letter from a mother who enclosed a list of all the things that her two-and-a-half-year-old son 'would not do'. The list was as follows:

a) come into the house after being in the garden
b) put on or take off his coat
c) stop touching ornaments or other items
d) stop opening cabinet drawers
e) come into the house after a shopping trip
f) leave the car after an outing

She told me that if she remonstrated with him he went into a terrible rage and viciously bumped his head on whatever was nearest – concrete, walls or doors. She was at the end of her tether.

Her little boy was obviously at the end of his tether as well with a mother who hadn't ever thought of looking at the world through his eyes. A child who has only lived for two and a half years has no idea that ornaments are precious and might be broken – they should be put in a safe place until he is a few years older – and the cabinets should have childproof catches. If he doesn't want to come in from the garden then he should be allowed to stay there and he certainly shouldn't be expected to take off his coat – it's very difficult to take a coat off when you're only two. At this age she should put it on and take it off again. If he doesn't want to come out of the car and is strapped in his seat then why not leave him there? If he is not strapped in then she will have to remove him forcibly because you cannot leave a small child at large in a car. I told her that he would be very angry but she would have to be firm for his own safety.

This little boy had been bossed about and corrected and given so many orders that he was actually putting up a 'fence' and when she wanted him to do something he was refusing. On principle he was doing exactly the opposite of what she wanted because he could never make his own decisions and was always being forced to do or not do certain things. She was trying to structure his whole life and he was rebelling; he'd probably got her temperament and these two very strong characters were fighting it out.

The more you say 'No' to a child the more he wants to do it, and it becomes a challenge to him. It's survival – going forward all the time, not being put off because somebody says 'No'. Usually you say 'No' because you don't want the child to hurt himself, but he doesn't understand that; to him it is just a challenge that needs to be met, so you must avoid having to say 'No' to

your child. I told the mother to try not to get
angry with her son, and that she was causing the
problems by being so angry with such a little
baby. She had made him very frustrated or he
wouldn't be banging his head and from now on
she had to try to be calmer with him or he would
go on from one problem to another.

The third Golden Rule

✦ Help your child feel secure
(Create a calm atmosphere)

I'm sure everybody wants their children to be happy
but of course human nature is such that no one is entirely happy all the time. You always make sure your
children have good food, warm clothes and all the
essentials in life, but there will be many moments when
they squabble, when they fight, when they don't want
to go to school because there is a bully. There are all
sorts of things that crop up that you will have to sort
out and the children must be able to feel that you are
there to put it right.

Let him know you're on his side

For instance, supposing your child has a visitor and the
interloper is very keen on your child's favourite toy but
your child is sad because it is the toy which goes with
him everywhere. In which case the awful remark, 'You
must share,' must not be used. You must be on your

child's side and you can say to him, 'Oh, isn't he kind – he likes holding teddy,' and then you must say to the interloper, 'Please give it back to James, because you see it is his very favourite toy.' If you appeal to a child's better nature you nearly always get your own way. Your child is very little and cannot be expected to know that when the other child leaves that toy won't go with him. Your child must know that you are his best friend and he can rely on you always.

Enjoy the present

It is impossible to make a child develop faster than he is able to, so you should enjoy him as he is. If you don't, he can feel your frustration with him and that in turn will make him frustrated and feel put down.

People are always trying to push their children ahead saying or thinking, for example, 'He can do his own shoes now' – all the time urging them forward to adulthood, which I find very sad because the years do fly and children should be allowed to have their childhood without being pushed. It should be a happy time. You too should savour every moment because there comes a moment when you think, Well, where did the years go? He's being very difficult, it was lovely when he was little. With the first child you can understand – new parents have never had a baby so they are longing for him to sit up or walk or whatever, but try not to do that. Try to live in the present as that is a very secure situation (see also The fourth Golden Rule, page 37).

Children need parents who are in agreement
I've met several families where the parents had different views about childcare, which is understandable as everyone has different views about everything, but dealing with a small live person you should try to compromise. It is difficult for the child if one parent has a very aggressive approach towards him and says, 'He must do as he is told,' and the other says, 'He is only two.' The child picks up from the atmosphere that the parents are in disagreement – and about him. So I think parents have to try to discuss their views without the child there and come to an agreement to meet each other halfway because the happiness of the child is paramount; it makes a child very uncertain and rather worried if each parent behaves differently towards him. I think it is easier if one person appears to be in charge and makes the decisions, so the father can say, 'We must ask Mummy.' My father was always very indulgent so I loved it if my mother was away for the day and he looked after me, but when she returned she was in charge and he would always defer to her.

Sometimes children do play parents off against each other and favour different parents at different times. You have to make the most of it and not get annoyed.

I once heard from parents – a mother who was heavily pregnant and getting very tired and a father who was feeling rejected – whose three-year-old daughter had decided she wanted

Mummy all the time and didn't want her father to do anything for her; if he tried to help she threw a tantrum.

I told the mother that children often insist on one particular person doing things for them. They want Mummy all the time and then for no apparent reason she will be spurned and they will want Daddy all the time. It does not mean anything though. I told the father not to feel offended. If he says, very casually, 'All right, Mummy do it then,' and appears not to mind either way she may well ask for Daddy to do it a minute later.

I said I thought the child could tell that at that moment Mummy didn't really want to do it. As she is three her mother could very gently say, 'Oh, please let Daddy do it, I am terribly tired.' If it is something she needs to do desperately, such as go to the loo, she will go with her father.

Keepers must agree too

It also worries me when children have a series of different people caring for them or in charge of them. Because I looked after my children for so long, they only ever had one keeper, but in some families whenever I went on holiday temporary nurses looked after my children and of course, promoted their own views. I remember once returning from holiday to find the elder child sitting nervously blinking and the younger one sitting on the sofa saying quietly, 'She kept on hitting me.' It was terrible for them – and heartbreaking for me. If a child has too many keepers, or keepers with different ideas on childcare, he becomes withdrawn since he's so unsure what the adult's response is going to be.

Keep your word

As far as possible you must always keep to your word. Occasionally when you can't then you must explain. If you tell your child you will take him to the zoo, or whatever, and you just can't do it, then you must say, 'I'm so sorry we can't go to the zoo today as Daddy's not feeling very well and we have to stay and look after him. We'll go another day.' So many people treat their children like sub-species but they're really just adults who haven't lived very long and must be treated with respect. From the minute they draw breath they are learning something every day.

Any little rule you have you must stick to as well. If you are terribly keen that the child shouldn't eat an inordinate amount of chocolate – just a little chocolate bar on Saturday – then you must be consistent. If well-meaning friends call and bring the child sweets or chocolates then you must say, 'Thank you very much for the Smarties. We'll keep them for Saturday. We'll put them in the little box where we keep the chocolate.' Children will accept that that is the rule.

People do give in for a peaceful life because all that

screaming and shouting does wear you down, but it is so much better in the long run if you don't.

One mother told me she was scared of her two-and-a-half-year-old son snapping at her. She thought that he could tell that she found him difficult and was avoiding her gaze and so she felt insecure and tended to give in to please him. He was very unhappy at the time, having just had a sibling.

I told her it was just a phase and he would soon grow out of it and they would be friends again. I said that she could occasionally ask his advice so they can try and be chums. In the bread shop, for example, she could say, 'Shall we buy some scones today?' I said that on the whole it is unhappy children who have problems. If a new baby has come to live in his house then that is a problem for a two-year-old and so she should stick up for him as much as possible but try not to handle him differently for fear of a tantrum. If she has to be firm then she should be firm without being unkind and do what she thinks is right.

The fourth Golden Rule

✦ Don't undermine your child's confidence
(Aim to build it up)

Never compare your child to anyone else's – everyone is a different person. I've heard people say to children, 'Susie Brown can tie her own shoelaces, can't you yet?' which of course is a terrible thing to say because some children are very dextrous and some children like doing up their shoelaces. Adults put children down all the time and squash and ridicule them, often saying, if you've been helping a child cut up his food, for example, 'Can't he do it himself?' It's belittling the child as if the child ought to be able to do it. Some children can't catch a ball, but don't remind your child that he can't. Sometimes solemn little children are worried and anxious that they can't do something and they try so hard. It would be better if you didn't do any ball throwing with him until he's older and can do it.

Your child is an individual
If your child enjoys putting on his own shoes then that is a game for him and that's fine, but otherwise do them for him. I always dress a child until he is at least five, unless he doesn't want me to. I always take things very slowly and I always help children do things unless they positively want to do it themselves. Children on the whole don't say 'No' to a bit of help. Children take a

long time to dress themselves and if you've always let them do it and you are suddenly in a hurry it is a cause of great frustration for them that you now want to help.

A child does what he is capable of doing, it is only when he is older that he achieves things through trying. Once a child has turned five then praising him is terribly important. Until then praise means very little, he has done something because it was fun and he was able to do it, it's something that has happened. He is doing what he is able to do; it's not at all like a child striving to get all his sums right. So a child who is in those developing years doesn't need a lot of praise, or criticism, he needs acceptance. Of course it is always nice to encourage a child and when they get to the stage of liking to jump off the bottom step of the stairs I might say, 'Jolly good, what a big jump,' but no more.

Neither praise nor criticise – accept

A two-year-old taking off his coat and throwing it on the floor I would neither praise for taking it off – he has reached that stage in his development – nor would I scold for throwing it on the floor. I would simply pick it up or I might stand by the cupboard and say, 'Would you pass it to me, please, so I can hang it up,' or you could put a special hook at his height for him to hang it up on – if he wants to. At this age a child copies everything so he might want to hang it up, but again I wouldn't praise him. He hung up the coat because he enjoyed doing so. A parent might praise the child for hanging up his coat and then the next day when he doesn't want to do it – he's done it once, he's bored with that game now – say, 'Well, you did it yesterday – why aren't you doing it today?' sounding cross. This might put the child off doing it again for a long time. He had done it in the first place because he was able to do it, but he hasn't lived long enough to understand that for ever after that coat has got to be put on that hook. He may be so intrigued that he keeps on doing it, but he may not.

I find it far better not to give a toddler any responsibility because even hanging a coat up can drive you mad because he takes so long and you are getting more and more impatient and so you try to help, which can start a tantrum.

Leave your child alone to discover
For me a child is a person, an individual in his own right, so I don't always tell him what to do or not to do but in his world I let him make his own decisions, up to a point. I always feel that play belongs to the child – he should be allowed to play with his toys how he wants to and work out in his own imagination how best to do things without being told. Of course I play games with children such as Ludo or Snap or football or playing shops which need a partner, but anything that is made as a toy for children then I leave them to it to work out as part of their development.

Children really do need, and enjoy, simple toys. From

two, children love bathing plastic dolls, which is water play, and very therapeutic. At this age, too, they get enormous fun out of playing with a ball. Of course when they get to be three they like fitting things in, like picture trays, and they do them over and over again but you must not show them how to do it. Produce the game with the board and the little pieces on the side – maybe leave three or four in – and let them work it out; that is very interesting for them.

I see lots of toys in the toy shop that can do lots of different things, but children like simple things so they can use their imagination a little. So many toys are too involved and too big – you find a baby's rattle and it is much bigger than the baby's hand which is so frustrating.

Follow your child's lead
I feel very strongly about children being given toys that are 'suitable' for their age and development. People are inclined to buy a toy for a slightly older age than the child as they think the child is bright and capable of more than his peers and because they want him to get on a little faster. This is foolish because a toy is meant to be played with and enjoyed; if you give a toy to a child who is not yet ready for it then he cannot get the intended play value out of it and becomes frustrated and angry and is set back rather than helped forward.

The effect is worsened because manufacturers are guilty of putting too young an age on toys. Most toy manufacturers put 'From age three' (for example) when it is only really suitable for a four-year-old; the enthusiastic parent or grandparent buys it for their 'bright' two-year-old who is quite unable to enjoy the toy and then of course there are tantrums and disappointments. The mother then tries to help by showing the child, which defeats the whole idea – the mother has discovered how to play with the toy but the child hasn't. By the time he is four, when he would really have appreciated being able to discover and master the toy for himself, he is bored with it.

A child given a toy that is too old for him will pick it up, take it out of its box and not do anything with it or throw the pieces about. If this happens, then once the child has gone to bed I would take the toy away and put it in a cupboard out of sight for six months and try again. If the same thing happens I would again remove it until such time as he is able to enjoy it. Don't feel disappointed with him – he will play with it when he is able.

Commands To Avoid

I have often heard busy parents and keepers issuing commands to children, putting them down and talking to them in a way that takes away their confidence. So this list is to be thought of as a reminder.

Avoid saying: 'Don't do that.'
Instead distract him: 'Oh, look at that shiny new car out of the window,' or 'What a beautiful drawing you've done here,' or 'Come on, let's put your coat on – we're going to the shops,' or 'Can I just ask you something?'

Avoid saying: 'Stay here,' 'Don't touch,' and so on.
Instead: Make your home and outdoor life as safe and child-friendly as possible.

Avoid saying: 'You're not a baby any more.'
Instead say: 'Of course you can sit in the pram/suck your thumb/go in the high chair,' or ignore it altogether.

Avoid saying (or even thinking): 'Oh, he's twenty-four months, he ought to be able to do that.'
Instead say: 'Well done, you.'

Avoid saying: 'I think my child is so cruel/mean/selfish/annoying.'
Instead think and say: 'I think my child is wonderful.'

Avoid saying: 'Put your shoes on!' 'Wash your hands!'
Instead: Put the shoes on for the child or take a flannel and wash his hands without talking about it.

Avoid saying: 'You're a naughty girl/boy.'
Instead say: 'You're a wonderful girl/boy.'

Avoid saying: 'Would you like to put your coat on?' (Begs the answer 'No.')
Instead say: 'Let's put on your coat and go to the shops now so we'll have time to play your favourite game when we get back.' Or, just put his coat on.

Avoid saying: 'If you hurt Toby's face you can't go to the zoo this afternoon.'
Instead say: 'Please don't throw that at Toby because it is rather hard and might hurt his face.'

Avoid saying: 'Janet, you must share your toys.'
Instead say: 'Please give it back to Janet, because it is her very favourite toy.'

Avoid saying: 'Can't she do it herself yet?'
Instead: Just do it for her – a child does what he can do.

Avoid saying: 'Phoebe, say "Thank you/Please."'
Instead say: 'Thank you so much for the lovely party,

Mrs Brown. Phoebe did enjoy it.'

Avoid saying: 'Can't you untie your shoelace?'
Instead say: 'Oh, isn't it tricky – I can't do it either.
Let me see.'

Avoid saying: 'Put that paintbrush down, we're going
to the shops now.'
Instead say: 'Oh, that's absolutely lovely. When we
get back from the shops you must do some more painting then we can give it to Granny. We'll put it safely in
the middle of the table so it won't be disturbed.'

Don't say: 'Hold my hand! It's a busy road.'
Instead: Just reach down and take his hand to cross
the road.

Don't say: 'Get off the table at once!'
Instead say: 'Oh, please don't sit there because you
might fall and bang your head, and in any case the
table is for eating off not for sitting on. Let's get out
that box of beads and you can thread them for me.'

Avoid saying: 'It's bed-time.'
Instead say: 'Come on, we'll blow some bubbles in
the bath.'

Avoid saying 'No' at any time.

CHAPTER THREE

Avoiding Tantrums

I WONDER IF CAVEMEN HAD TANTRUMS? MAYBE IT'S THE pace we live at, with so many frustrations and aspirations that go wrong. You don't always know what has frustrated the child, although you might have a good idea. You probably think it isn't worth making all that fuss about, but it is to the child.

Reach him before the tantrum does
Even in the happiest of homes, some children have tantrums and some don't. You can't avoid tantrums altogether but you can try to make the child feel that everything is all right and that he is understood no matter how he behaves. By being on the child's side and trying to help him avoid situations that would normally frustrate him and might cause a tantrum, you can certainly help him. For instance, sometimes a toy that clicks together suddenly won't; then you can join in and say, 'Oh, isn't it tricky – I can't do it either. Let me see.'

Sometimes with the best will in the world you say, 'I'll help you do it,' and that very often makes him very cross because he would much rather try to do it himself. You just don't know exactly what will upset him. The child could be tired or hungry, and you know that if something is difficult to do then being under the weather always makes it worse. It's the same for a child.

Occasionally with children various foods produce allergies. For example, chocolate can result in an over-stimulated child and a very tense mother and a situation in which tantrums can easily occur. Do talk to your doctor if you feel your child might be allergic to any foods and suggest you try omitting these foods from your child's diet and monitoring him closely.

Everyone wants his own way

Small children would, if they could put it into words, want everything to be their way because they haven't lived long enough to know that they have to think of other people. As adults we're programmed to think of others, that's civilisation, but children aren't, so for them it is having to fit in that often sets off a tantrum. Often a child is playing happily when you have to collect an elder sibling from school and so you have to interrupt his play and remove him from a particular toy he is enjoying. With a such a young child you cannot reason because he doesn't understand reasoning. As an adult you have to intervene in the child's world when it is time to eat, or go out, or go to bed, or to stop him doing anything that may harm himself or others. But I try never to tell children to do or not to do things, so that they feel I'm intervening as little as possible (see Chapter Two). It isn't easy to do this in a busy household but it is worth thinking about. Imagine always having someone telling you to do or not to do things. Of course you have to do certain things, for example your shopping before the shops close, but we learn as time goes by how to cope with that and fit it into our routine. But for a child to have someone say, 'Put that down, we're going to the shops now,' is a cause of great frustration and the less of it you can do the better. Children should be frustrated as little as possible which is jolly difficult because the pace of life is designed for you rather than for the child.

Tantrums are based on frustration for which there are different causes: whether they're not allowed to eat something, not allowed to do something, can't do something or whatever. The different commands below are ones most of us have heard ourselves use – I hope I have managed to illustrate alternative, and better, ways of getting the same results.

'Come on. It's time for bed!'

By the time a child is nearing two he sometimes would rather not go to bed. He is beginning to rebel against decisions made for him and any kind of rule. Having accepted things, he is now forming a character and having his own ideas about what to do and when. At this age it becomes useful more or less to stick to a routine, which makes for a harmonious situation all round, but not to be so hidebound that you can't change things as and when you want (see My Tried and Tested Routines, Chapter Six). If you have a regular night-time routine which forms part of the day then bed-time is a very happy time (see Four Golden Rules, Chapter Two). But if you haven't yet established a routine there comes a moment when the child says, 'I don't want to go to bed,' and, of course, he has a point because if he hasn't always gone at the same time then he feels he has a choice. At that point you either have to be very firm and say, 'It is time you had a bath and went to bed. I'm very busy and now's the time,' or, preferably, you could be chummy and say, 'Come on, we'll blow some bubbles in the bath.' It is more effective to distract a child of this age when you want something to happen rather than to keep insisting – make a suggestion rather than give an order – or they may start a tantrum which is best avoided.

'You can only play for a few minutes'

Children live in the present so can't think, I'm going to bed soon, or It's lunchtime soon, or Oh, it's nearly six o'clock. I'd better get on and finish this puzzle before bedtime. Children really have no sense of time and so they can't hurry up with a game, knowing that they will have to go out or whatever very soon. So if they say,

'Can I paint now?' it's not fair to say, 'Yes, but we've only got a few minutes,' because it means nothing to them. Then it is frustrating for them to stop painting when they have only just started and who can blame them. And who can blame the mother for expecting the child to fit in with her routine when he's got his own ideas.

People say, 'Well the world can't revolve round the child,' and of course it can't, the child has to fit in. But my aim is to make the fitting-in a happy and comfortable experience for the child. If the child were painting I would say, 'Oh, that's absolutely lovely. When we get back you must do some more then we can hang it on the wall. We'll put it safely in the middle of the table so it won't be disturbed.' By saying that I have implied that he will be going out but also coming back and that he can do more because what he is doing is so lovely. He won't exactly understand what is happening, but he will have a picture in his mind of what the afternoon is going to be like.

'We have to go out now'

Another way of making fitting-in seem not so bad is if you manage to fit in an errand for you with some fun for the child. If a child has just started a particular game and you say, 'Come on, let's go out and buy the sausage rolls,' then you know they are going to be angry so it is a good idea to add something to please them like: 'We'll take the ball to kick in the park.'

'You must come home now!'
One of my little girls would scream and scream when she had to leave a particular family after tea – she enjoyed being there so much. Sometimes it is tempting to stay and have a drink with the kind mother who is offering you one and then the child can play for a little longer, but the child will have to leave anyway and staying a bit longer can make it even more difficult to leave.

I was once contacted by a mother who told me her five-year-old sometimes went to visit friends after school. When she collected him there was always the most frightful fuss: 'Mummy I hate you. Go away! I don't want to go with you!' She didn't know how to get him home.

I told her that this is one of the times when she has to be firm. It is six-ish and bed-time for both children so it is no use dilly-dallying. A firm hand on the wrist and lead him out of the door with his coat in your hand. 'Come on, Tommy, time to go. Thank you very much, Mrs So and so. See you another day.' If he is very reluctant to leave behind a particular toy he has been playing with I would sometimes ask if we could borrow it for the night and then I would return it the next day.

I said that the mother should not threaten her child, saying he can't come again or forbidding future treats, because all this is happening at the moment and all the things you are forbidding are in the future. The child can't think like that: his existence is entirely in the present. If a child has been at school all day and then has gone out for tea and is playing with different toys he is probably over-tired as it has been a long and exciting day and he needs to come home and go to bed.

I avoid continually telling children what to do and what not to do, but this is one of the times when you must be in charge. I am doing this not to be mean or to assert my authority but because the child needs to have a bath and go to bed. Everybody with children knows that if a child is over-tired he is extremely difficult to cope with and, of course, he is not very happy.

'Stop! Come back and hold my hand!'

Other times when one has to be firm and in control are when one can see a dangerous situation: for example, if the child picks up a sharp knife or starts crossing a road. For children's safety and security one has to be one step ahead of them. There might not be any traffic coming but you must still hold their hand to cross the road. If a child likes walking along the street without holding my hand, that's fine, but when crossing over I'd just reach down and take his. Or, I put my child in reins (see page 28).

'Please behave, we're out visiting'

Temper tantrums are often the result of an atmosphere created by a tense and irritable parent, perhaps at a particularly stressful time, such as Christmas, when the child is extremely excited and excitable anyway. The parent has so many things on her mind and so much to do and is curt with the child, which results in an unhappy child having a tantrum.

Often the tenseness and irritability of the parent is worse when out visiting. I have heard of several incidents where the family has had to leave granny, for example, because the child has 'misbehaved' and had 'tantrum after tantrum'. Visiting or staying with friends or relations can anyway be a tense time for parents as they are not only trying to be helpful and obliging themselves, but also anxious that the child should behave and 'make a good impression'. The child is excited to be in a new house with different people and yet can feel the parent's tension, or sometimes even be at the brunt of it, and it is a situation which can easily produce tantrums with the parent and child getting on each other's nerves and the atmosphere spiralling downhill.

'We have to get ready now!'

You often have children dawdling over getting dressed before breakfast because the child is still a little sleepy. If you have to go out then you must be a little firm. Instead of letting them get themselves dressed, which can take a long time, I would simply do it for them. It is another time when you must be in charge, as it were.

I received a letter from a mother about her two-year-old daughter who just screamed and screamed as her mother was dressing her in the morning. Her mother said, 'She is so strong and strong-willed that I am at my wits' end.'

I said that children do very often resent having their night-clothes taken off and other clothes put on. It is amazing how strong children are and if they do not want their clothes on it can be quite a battle, so you have to use your strength against the child. You must resist getting angry or slapping the child. If you do, in a way the child has won because he has driven you to lose your temper. And afterwards you will regret it.

I remember going in to one of my girls' bedrooms and she was still in her nightie. She said, 'Are we going skating?' and I replied, 'How can we? It's already nine o'clock and your lesson starts in half an hour.' I've never seen anyone get dressed so fast, but she was around eight or nine years old. As children get older I put the ball in their court and if they want to do something at a specific time then the onus is on them to be ready for it. But when they are little it is quite different.

'Hurry up!'
It is extraordinary but children can feel in the atmos-

phere that you are in a hurry. Often one has been with a
child who is three-ish and you want to get him into the
pushchair but he wants to push it so you try to lift him
into the pushchair. To make things more difficult, he
goes all rigid and you have to use all your strength to lift
him and quickly fasten the straps so he can't get out.
You are battling with your child and you feel rather a
fool, but you have to get somewhere on time, maybe to
pick the older sibling up. On such occasions it is important not to lose your temper and get angry and shout,
but to appear to be keeping calm even if you are
anxious about being late. I have seen desperate mothers
slapping their children and who can blame them, but
you must try to avoid this because you'll be so fed up
with yourself later on in the evening.

Better still, don't lift the child into the pushchair but
try to call his bluff. I remember once having a situation
like that and I said to the child, 'All right, walk!' We
walked at top speed, me holding his hand so he was
almost running and then after several, 'You're going too
fast, you're going too fast,' I could say, 'Well, get in the
chair then,' and he was very relieved to do so.

In an ideal world it is of course best to be very well
organised so there is no rushing, but life with a small
child, not to say two or three small children, is hectic.
They have separate lives and no idea of time so you
have to try and fit everything in with as little fuss as
possible.

'You can't go on the swings today'

I often see children having tantrums when they have been forbidden to go on those giraffes, or elephants that you put a coin in to move. When the coin is used up and the machine stops working they get very angry and want it to go on rocking, being too young to understand that their time is over. All my children have been on these machines but they have all been old enough to know that you put a coin in to make it work, then the money runs out and you have to get off. They may rock backwards and forwards a little afterwards to see if it will restart, but they are over three and understand things more.

When our children went to the park we never took them out of the pram until they were two so only then did they go on the swings. If you put a younger child on the swings you do create problems. There is something about swinging that small children absolutely love and of course there is no harm in them having a little swing but if you put a child under two in a swing then every time he sees one anywhere he wants a go and can't understand why you won't let him. They then make a lot of fuss, so to avoid arguments it is best to wait until they're old enough to understand.

Before we went out the children would always know that we were 'Going to the swings' and then we went for the morning and that was fine, but if we were going to the park and saw the swings then we didn't go on them unless we'd planned to. I would say, 'Oh, aren't

they lovely, we must come oneorning and go on them.'
If you always make 'No' mean 'No' and 'Yes' mean 'Yes'
then children over a certain age will accept it.

'Sssshhh . . . . you have to be quiet'

I do find that people introduce children to situations
and toys far beyond their understanding, things that
they would get so much fun out of a little bit later. I still
see people in the street with a little child in a pushchair
who has been given a wind-up toy but who is far too
young to understand what to do with it (see Chapter
Two). People take children to museums, theatres,
cinemas, the zoo and so on when they are still far too
small. At first they are rather fascinated but they then
very quickly become bored. Such treats should be
reserved until the children are older and know what
they are going to see and can look forward to it.

There are various situations for which you have to
monitor and prepare children. For instance, taking small
children to visit relations in hospital is very bewildering
for them and is often best avoided.

I once heard from a lady whose husband had
been in hospital for a few days and was likely to
be there for longer. She had visited him with their
two-year-old son who had enjoyed the visit and
then had had the most enormous tantrum (his
first) as they were leaving. She now didn't know
whether to take her son to see his father again.

I told her that I would never take a two-year-old child to hospital. Instead when her son had asked, 'Where's Daddy?' I would just have replied, 'He's in hospital to have his leg made better.' I wouldn't have volunteered any more information and I don't think the child would have asked to go and see Daddy. People do take children to hospital with the best intentions, but don't understand how upsetting it can be for them, seeing Daddy in bed in hospital, while they have to go home to bed. For the same reason I never like children to go to hospital to see their mothers when they have just had a new baby.

'Let me help you'

I've seen tiny children given large knives and forks at table, sitting on an adult chair and they really can't manage them. If a toddler asks for a large knife and fork like an older child then you can say, 'Why don't you try?' but otherwise I always give a child a teaspoon until he is almost four, when I give him a small fork. It is only when a child is five that I give him a full-size knife and fork and show him how to use them, and if he finds it difficult then I just take them away again. It is so frustrating for a child to have utensils which are far too big for him; yet if you offer to help that can create further frustrations for him. If you see a child struggling then I find the best thing to do is simply to lean over him without saying anything, cut his food up and then, again without saying anything, just put his usual spoon into the food. That way he can start eating with it.

Often an offer of help, a remark or a slight criticism can trigger off a tantrum – it is best to keep your own counsel. Sometimes at the table if children are having difficulties spearing the meat or picking up the last spoonful and you offer to help them it makes them so mad – they throw the spoon down and shout as if to say, 'I wish they'd mind their own damn business.' The same thing can happen if they are playing with a toy and you butt in to show them how to wind it up or they are trying to do up a zip or a button and you offer to help. If you are in a great hurry say, 'I'll have to do your buttons quickly because we are terribly late and haven't got spare time,' and just do them and hope it won't lead to a storm. Or else you could put the ball in their court and ask, 'Do you mind if I do your buttons today because we are rather late?' and hope that they will kindly allow you to do them.

'You always wear this shirt – what's wrong with it?'

At this stage in a child's life he likes everything always to be the same no matter what it is: food, toys, the day's routine. Children feel very secure if things are always the same, but of course there are small changes sometimes (either deliberate or inadvertent) which make them quite angry. Any little routine, the order in which you put their clothes on, or always having breakfast in a certain pair of slippers, will have to be the same day after day. They may also remember what trousers they wore with that same shirt previously; you will have forgotten, but they will have remembered and will want to wear the shirt with exactly the same trousers as last time. Often you think they are protesting because they don't like that particular shirt when what they are trying to say is that they want to wear it as part of the same ensemble as last time. This frustration can lead to tantrums.

If a child has an obsession about something then it is far easier and kinder to fall in with it because more often than not it will be over fairly quickly. However, if it is opposed then it develops into an enormous problem.

I once met a little three-year-old boy whose mother had bought him a Thunderbird outfit for his birthday and he was so taken with it, he absolutely lived in it. If there was an occasion when he couldn't wear it he insisted on wearing something blue because it was the same colour as the Thunderbird outfit. It was driving his mother mad because he was going to inherit the summer wardrobe of an older brother in which there was nothing blue and so he was making a terrible fuss and refusing to wear any of the clothes.

I suggested that she bought him a couple of pairs of cheap blue shorts and T-shirts which would please him, so she did. A few months later he had worn the blue, was fed up with it and now was happy to wear anything. If the mother had been casual about the whole thing and when he had said, 'I don't want to wear that, I want a blue T-shirt,' she had immediately said, 'Oh, let's go and buy one,' then it would never have been a problem. He would have been thrilled to choose the T-shirt in blue and then almost the next day he would have forgotten about wanting to wear blue. By trying to make him forget about wanting to wear blue it had become an issue, which the parents discussed in front of him and was blown up out of all proportion.

I told the mother that sometimes it is almost as though children are testing you – it is their will against yours. They want to stake their claim and if you go along with a child then he has nothing to rebel against. The mother had resisted, which was a form of aggression, so it was a battle of wills. Once she bought the blue clothes in a way he had won, but by conceding she had won because the battle was then over. I told her that in Germany there is an expression, 'The cleverer person gives in.' Giving in is not a sign of weakness, but a sign of strength. It shows you have the sense to give in, knowing that it is something unimportant and not worth fighting about.

Parents always feel they must win every argument because they are anxious to show their child who is boss, but by fighting a tiny child you are simply showing your fear and demonstrating to your child that you think aggression is the way forward. Remember that the child is a person in his own right, a separate personality altogether and you can really only frustrate him by insisting he does certain things you think he ought to do. Obviously there are times when you have to enforce your will but make sure that what you are trying to do or say is essential. If not, why not let your child develop in his own way?

'But I've just given you the red mug'

If you have a collection of mugs and sometimes the child has one mug and sometimes another then it gives him the idea that he can always have a different one. So if you give the child the red mug and he makes a great fuss and says, 'I want the blue mug,' it is difficult to know whether he really minds about not having the blue mug or whether he is frustrated by something else and the mug is the first thing to take against, as it were. It could also be a frustration that someone has taken for granted which mug he should have when he wanted to choose. Of course a child can't think about it as deeply as that but sometimes he doesn't want to accept what is given to him: he makes a fuss and then he gets what he wants and has a feeling of power – and why not? But I would never ask the child which mug he wanted because it would just confuse him – wait for him to protest, if that is what he wants to do.

'I just want to wash your hair – that's all'

I've had many queries from parents whose children, usually four-year-olds, did not want their hair brushed or washed or cut. Certainly with cutting, a small child must be fearful sitting in a chair with somebody wielding a pair of scissors round his head. Some children do mind very much and they are distraught, worried, frightened and quite often scolded for their feelings. If a child is afraid of the hairdresser then I would leave him for as long as possible without a haircut. Then, when it was absolutely essential to cut it, I would wash his hair in the bath and give him a toy to play with and then comb his hair and snip away a little bit at it myself. Or if you are nervous about cutting his hair yourself, maybe you could ask a friendly hairdresser to come to your home. I always snip children's hair in the bath until they are five or six and if they have been to the hairdresser with me then they know what to expect and will happily let the hairdresser cut their hair.

*O*ne mother who contacted me said her four-year-old daughter had always hated having her thick hair brushed. Even when her mother had given her quite a short bob for a haircut she still minded. Her mother thought her daughter must have a very sensitive scalp. She had tried singing songs and telling stories and all sorts of different brushes but nothing worked, her daughter still screamed hysterically and her three-year-old sister was now copying her elder sister's behaviour. They both hated having their hair washed too.

I told the mother that her hair had to be washed and brushed and as all things pass, she wouldn't mind as much next year. She should get the brushing and the washing over and done with as quickly as possible and not sing songs and tell stories, but just be very quick and firm – not cross, but just get on with it.

Washing a child's hair should always be done as quickly as possible. If a child makes a great fuss – and most do go through a phase where they mind having it done – you can try holding a slightly moist flannel tightly over the child's eyes to stop the water getting in (let the child hold the flannel once he gets older), or ask them to look at the ceiling so their head is back, or you could use those 'brims' that you get from the chemist which I think are a very good invention. Once children get older they can lie down in a shallow bath so they wet their hair themselves and look like that Millais picture of Ophelia floating in the river. It's a chore that can't be avoided so you have to get on with it and they have to get used to it.

'You're going to hurt yourself'

Lots of parents issue commands that frustrate a child and often cause a tantrum: 'Get down off the table!', 'Stop climbing on the wall!' or 'Leave those scissors alone!'

The above situations are all potentially dangerous, so you have to appeal to a child's good sense and if that doesn't work, then you have to be very firm – what you might call cross without being angry. A very small child of two does not know about breaking legs so I would just lift him off the table and remove whatever he has stood on to get on the table. I would be as calm as possible and as I was lifting him off the table I would say something to divert him. If he was determined to keep climbing then I would remove everything around the table. It is no use saying 'No' to a child of that age because for him it is a challenge to try and get on to the table. It is all part of his development and it is a period of his life which won't last very long. He may well be very annoyed at being removed from the table but it has to be done.

If the child is three and climbing on the table then you must appeal to his better nature and say something like, 'Oh, please don't do that because you might fall and bang your head, and in any case the table is for eating off not for sitting on. Let's get out those crayons and you can draw a picture for me.' I think by that age it is a child who is slightly bored who is climbing on the table. If he refuses to come off then again you have to lift him off as it is dangerous. Be prepared for him being cross.

'Don't touch those jars – we're not going to buy them'

This is the sort of thing you should never say before a child has touched the jars because he might not have thought of touching them and you are giving him the idea of doing so. I have seen people in shops shouting 'Don't touch those' and so the child goes and does exactly that and it's one up to them. If your two-year-old has already touched them then I would just take his hand away from the jars without saying anything and walk along holding his hand firmly. At that moment you have to avoid a catastrophe, and if you walk with him away from the jars there probably won't be any trouble. It is important not to be aggressive or to shout. At that age it is so much better if children can be on reins or in a pushchair or in the supermarket trolley where you can keep an eye on them.

It is of course a great help if you can leave your small child with a friend or relation rather than take him to the supermarket because you will get on better and faster without him. If he has to come with you, once he is older he can help – it can become a bit of a game, asking him to get that piece of cheese or whatever you need. But it can be exhausting and taxing on your imagination.

'No, you can't have a toy'

When I was a child we used to go to the toy shop and never even thought that the toys were for sale. We just enjoyed looking at all the lovely toys. We never asked to have anything, but then we had never been bought anything from a toy shop while we were there so it never occurred to us that the toys were for sale. In an ideal world if you never buy anything for your child while you are in a shop then that is best for both you and the child. It is fun for the child because then he can just enjoying looking – like in an art gallery – and is not constantly wondering, Shall I have this? Or shall I rather have that? He can enjoy things for what they are. It is extremely difficult to discourage this grab, grab, grab attitude because other children get things and tell your children, but if you never buy them anything at the shops then they never ask.

Even if you have always bought your child something in the past you can still start to make a stand: you could say to the child, 'It's too expensive,' or 'You've already got one,' and I've always said, 'Well, the things are really meant for Christmas or birthdays.' If the child is very small and has been used to having things then he will make a scene, but if he's a little bit older you can say, 'We can't buy it today because I haven't got enough money with me.' If he is very keen you could say, 'Would you like it for your birthday?' A two-year-old will have a tantrum or two but you must make a stand and keep calm and quite soon he will realise that he isn't going to get anything and will stop asking.

'You have far too many sweets'

If you're in a shop that sells sweets and chocolates and the child says, 'Oh, I'd like a chocolate bar,' and you say, 'No, you can't have one today, you had one yesterday. You have far too many sweets,' and that produces a tantrum, then I wouldn't buy him the chocolate afterwards because if you do it sets a pattern: every time you are in the sweet shop he gets some sweets or chocolate. On the next visit to the shop, he'll remember getting sweets last time and so will expect them again, and if he doesn't get them is likely to throw a tantrum.

I don't agree with those who think that a small child decides to have a tantrum as a means of persuading an adult to grant his wishes. Children live so much in the present , they don't think, If I have a tantrum they will give it to me, or even, Last time I had a tantrum they gave in to me so I'll try it again. They might think like that once they are four, but not when they are very small – tantrums are spontaneous expressions of anger.

'Say please . . .'

As a parent you should be striving for the child's happiness, not the fact that they have wonderful manners and say 'Please' and 'Thank you'. Of course that is nice, but it is an extra, not an essential. Children copy your behaviour and by the time they are five if you have basic good manners they will too. At that age you can sometimes remind them quietly (not in front of anyone else) what they are expected to do, but before then you really shouldn't worry about manners. To small children 'Thank you' are two words that have no meaning.

Certainly it is important that the child is thanked whenever he does something kind just as you would an adult. If you always say 'Please' and 'Thank you' to the child, and to others, then sooner or later he will pick up the habit and start doing it himself. I've heard people get absolutely furious with children if they don't say 'Thank you' after a party. If the child hears, 'Say thank you,' and 'Say please,' all the time then he is learning how to be bossy, not how to have good manners. It is aggression that is being pumped into him, not politeness.

Might A Child's Position In The Family Affect His Tantrums?

Most children have tantrums so I don't think that whether a child is the eldest, youngest or somewhere in the middle has anything to do with how many tantrums he has. But possibly what triggers off the tantrums might differ depending on the child's position in the family.

The firstborn

I do find that people with a first baby are not as spontaneous as parents with second and third children. The first baby is a new experience for the parents and so they are really having to feel their way. New parents are very often quite frightened of the baby and don't really know what to do; and they get so much conflicting advice that there can be a great deal of confusion. When a first baby cries they get worried and when he gets angry with them they get worried and possibly scared of what he is going to do next. Children are very aware of atmosphere and if you are positive in your approach to them then it spells security (see Chapter Two); if you are not quite sure how to cope with them then they can sense your uncertainty.

Even an only child can get frustrated and although he

is showered with love and affection he might well start having tantrums in the second year because that is what happens, it is part of his development almost as though he wants to let his parents know how angry he is.

Staking his claim once a sibling has arrived

I once met a family with a tiny boy and a baby sibling and this little boy broke everything and constantly did things to get his parents' attention – he was very angry. I suppose that could be called a tantrum, although it's not a 'basic tantrum', throwing himself on the floor, screaming and shouting. I think that on the whole eldest children have tantrums more than other children. They often start when the baby is made to stop being the baby because another one takes his place.

The first child is usually the demanding one because when he arrived in the family there were no other distractions for the parents – there was plenty of time to acknowledge the child's needs and he was very much king of the castle. So it is really quite difficult when number two comes along because, even with the best will in the world and the best parents, number one's demands may now well be ignored and turn into lots of tantrums. I had tantrums – I was the elder and was sometimes desperately unhappy and very angry. I had a sister who was very close in age to me and at the time I didn't like her. I think the elder child has to make a statement. He is very angry about the sibling who has arrived and even though my mother didn't particularly fuss over my sister, it didn't make any difference, there was another person there – my sister had moved in, like birds into a nest, and I had to get her out.

You do occasionally meet older children who are very kind to the younger siblings, but they are not the norm and to me it seems somewhat unnatural, almost as if being nice to the sibling is to please the parents so they will like him.

Middle children

The eldest child makes so many demands that the parents are always busy trying to fulfil them; the youngest child has the helplessness of being the youngest and gets looked after with no fuss; and in all this the middle child is more or less ignored, which could either make the child want to make his presence felt or could mean he has a more peaceful life with no tantrums.

With second and subsequent children the parents are much more relaxed, which of course is nature being clever in a way because often the second child is quite different from the first and the third from both of them and so on. If the first child has been very easy, the middle one can be very difficult or the other way round. Very often people enjoy the subsequent babies much more than the first one. I have also noticed a lot that with the first baby parents are very anxious for him to grow up whereas with the second and subsequent babies they hang on to them. Of course the second baby never has his parents all to himself although he accepts that because it is the situation he was born into. He also has the aggression of the older child to deal with, who might give him a poke and a pinch.

Youngest children

The only one of my children who never had a tantrum was the youngest child who was in some ways left more or less to grow up on his own without too much fussing. If the youngest child has any problems they will be different from those of the elder siblings because when he arrives they will already be there and may, or may not, welcome him. The parents are by now more used to children and so won't be as anxious as they were with number one and subsequent children. They will realise that everything is all right within reason and that children do have difficult times, but they are only phases, and won't pay much attention to the conflicting advice they are offered. There may also be a sibling who is old enough to be really kind and helpful to the little baby, in which case he will have someone a little bit taller than him helping him to put on his shoes or get into his high chair and so on. None the less, the youngest can sometimes have to put up with a lot of bossing from elder siblings, almost as if he has lots of parents, which can be hugely frustrating and can trigger off tantrums.

CHAPTER FOUR

During the Tantrum

THE OTHER DAY I SAW SOME THREE-YEAR-OLD children climbing along a window ledge inside a restaurant. It was so dangerous but their mothers ignored them. Their food was sitting on the table getting cold and yet they were being allowed to run around.

I wondered why their mothers didn't call them: were they afraid their children would make a scene? One can't help thinking that we have come to a pretty pass if mothers have become afraid that their children will make a scene if frustrated. It should be such a treat going to a restaurant to eat – but I would only take a child to a restaurant ideally once he was five, or maybe four if there was an older child in the family.

Having a tantrum in public

Children who have tantrums in public embarrass their parents enormously and people passing are either full of advice as to what to do or laugh and walk on. It is a terrible experience, however, and you have to try not to mind being the focus of everyone's attention, or you become more tense and the child does, too.

If you are in a restaurant or café I would take the child out until the tantrum is over: you are on the child's side but you cannot ruin other people's pleasure, although most people are so used to seeing children behaving badly nowadays that they keep on eating. If you are in a shop when the tantrum starts I would hold his hand very firmly and leave the shop – if you can – because you can't expect people in the shop not to mind. It can be difficult, though, if your child is strong, but you must try.

Once he has calmed down, if it is essential that you return then I would do so. Generally, however, I would take a child home after he has had a tantrum because he is probably tired or hungry.

How to cope
I used more or less to ignore it when one of my children had a tantrum. I would just hold his hand very firmly and keep walking and if there was a handy bench I would sit down and put the child on my knee and of course the tantrum would subside slowly and you would be able to wipe the tears.

Occasionally one does see a small child in the street hurl himself on the ground screaming and the mother is so embarrassed. It is difficult to pick up a child in that state, so you have to leave him to get it out of his system and just wait patiently. You fight a losing battle if you try to pick him up or hold his hand and try to drag him to his feet – children are so strong when they are having a tantrum. This is why people spank them but you should avoid that if at all possible.

Try not to get angry

This is one of those things that it is very easy to say, but it is very difficult for the person in charge to keep calm because the child is making a lot of noise and flinging himself about. The first thing that springs to mind is to take some action – to grab the child, or shake him and say, 'Stop doing that!' but that does not work, so you must aim to appear very calm. Inside you may think, Not another tantrum, but ignoring it as far as possible is really the best thing. Even if he says, 'I hate you,' during the tantrum, just ignore it or even reply , 'Well, I love you.' That takes the wind out of his sails a little bit. It helps children if you let them know you care for them no matter what they do or how they behave.

Do tantrums differ?

Like most things there are different levels of tantrum. A child can throw a tantrum which is over so quickly one might call it a mini-tantrum. He stamps his feet and shouts and afterwards it is almost as if he feels embarrassed because what was upsetting him isn't quite what he thought it was. For example, if you say to the child,

'We're going out later to see Grandma,' or anything the child really likes doing, and you later say, 'We can't go after all,' he starts kicking and screaming. Then you continue, 'Wait a minute, I was just going to say we'll be going to the swings instead,' then it's almost as though he feels rather foolish and quickly stops.

Then there are full-blown tantrums, when a child is almost out of control: typically they fling themselves on the floor and scream and fling out their arms and legs and drum their heels. I have also seen children jumping up and down in the air with both feet or lurching forward and biting things – usually something soft like a cushion, or a bedcover – and picking up things and hurling them, though not at anybody. I suppose that may be seen as symbolically throwing the anger away, but children won't recognise that. Sometimes children hit and kick their mothers during a tantrum and I have seen desperate people kick the child back or grab him by the shoulders and shake him. I can't really blame the parent but I would try not to respond like that.

I sometimes attempt to put my arms around a child having a tantrum, especially if he looks as if he might harm himself by scratching his knees on a gravelly path or banging his head against the wall. Usually they simply want to get on with it and have a good old tantrum, in which case I would let them. As it dies down they are so relieved to be cuddled as if they are thinking 'Thank goodness it's all over now'.

Breath-holding and head-banging tantrums

Where I was trained one of the boys held his breath until he lost consciousness and then collapsed and lay on the floor. We would pick him up and hold him closely and wipe his face with a cold, damp flannel and very soon he would recover. We would hold him for a few more minutes and then he carried on playing. He was a very quiet little boy and no one was being horrid to him but he just suddenly took against things, like being asked to put a bib on. Such behaviour happens very quickly but it is frightening, especially the first time you see it.

Other children bang their heads on the floor or any other available hard object. It is rather a curious thing to do because although it doesn't damage them it must hurt. Many children do it in their sleep: I knew one little boy who banged his head on the wall all night, and all one could do was move the bed so he wasn't near the wall. He had a wonderful nanny, but a very disturbed home life. When children are very angry they bang their heads so who's to say that if they bang their heads in their sleep they're not angry too? The strange thing is that most children never seem to injure themselves, although there are exceptions. I wonder if nature is telling them to do it to comfort themselves. It's almost like rocking. I've seen a little boy of eighteen months rhythmically rocking himself on the spot in the park, on his hands and knees. He too had a very unhappy home life.

However some children do bang their heads if they have earache so if your child can't yet talk and starts banging his head it is worth asking the doctor to have a look inside his ears.

Do you try to stop him having a tantrum?

The child can't help having a tantrum. Children have tantrums because they are rebelling against something they can't control, and feel inadequate because they can't change it. In a way they feel furious with themselves because they have too much responsibility, too much power and they can't deal with it. If something has really upset your child it may well automatically result in a tantrum. He hasn't lived long enough to say, 'Well, I won't make a fuss – it's not worth it,' or 'Tomorrow it will be better,' or 'Well, I won't have a tantrum because it won't help in the long run' – it's a spontaneous thing.

If I can see a tantrum starting then I do occasionally try to prevent it by diffusing the situation. I would try to distract the child by saying something that he wanted to hear such as, 'Now just stop shouting for a minute, just a minute, I wanted to say, "Instead of going to the park we're going to the shops for Mama,"' and it would either stop his tantrum permanently or just for a minute, after which he would start again.

During the tantrum

Once the tantrum has started I never interfere. The child has a reason for having a tantrum and you don't know what it is; in a way the tantrum is a sort of safety valve – he has a good old shout and stamp of the feet and then it's all over. I have heard of people pouring water on the child's head but I think that is a barbaric thing to do. I have heard of others whispering to try to stop the tantrum but I think whispering would be ineffective – if he feels like having a tantrum then why not let him? He needs to get something out of his system. I always either stay in the room and get on with whatever I am doing without commenting on the tantrum or I wander next door but stay close enough so I am there when he has finished his tantrum in case he needs me. I never fuss over the child and I don't pick him up and hold him unless he is about to kick the glass cabinet door or we are outside, when I want to get him out of the way of people's feet. Otherwise, holding a child down when he is in the middle of a tantrum is a very aggressive thing to do.

Do I leave the child alone to have his tantrum?

I've heard people say that if you walk away while a child is having a tantrum it will stop because he has no audience, but I think he will keep on having the tantrum and whatever has made him angry will still be making him angry. He won't think 'I'm going to stop now there is no one here to watch me'. He may run after you and hang on to you and either put his arms around you or perhaps kick your shins. If he were old enough and could dissect why he was having this tantrum I think he would be so pleased that you were there and you were not angry and the tantrum might then tail off. If you have the time I always think it is best to stay quietly with the child and observe what is happening, but not interfere. If you are very angry it is best to leave the room because you might lose your temper and spank him very hard which might stop the tantrum, but you would regret it, so it is best to leave the scene of the crime, as it were.

I have known people put the child in another room and close the door and in a way that does give the person in charge time to have a deep breath and calm down. The child will be livid and kick the door but when the anger is released and the tantrum is over then he will come in quietly for his cuddle. I think if your child is a hurler then you may have to take him to a room where there is nothing he can break to have his tantrum. Or some people put the child in his cot as somewhere safe to have a tantrum. You would probably stay with him but if you had to run down and answer the doorbell then he would be safe in the cot and he would probably lie down and suck his thumb or go to sleep. But I would only recommend it if I were very busy or had to see somebody or make an important telephone call.

Protecting siblings

If the younger child has taken a precious toy belonging to the older child and won't let go, then the older child does sometimes have a mini-tantrum and push the younger one over. I would pick the younger child up because I don't want him to be injured, but I wouldn't get angry. I might just say 'Oh, don't do that – it hurts him,' but otherwise I would try to be quiet. If the child having the tantrum shows signs of attacking the sibling then you must make sure that he can't do so, but in my experience it is the person in charge that the child is angry with, rather than the sibling.

CHAPTER FIVE

After the Tantrum

SOMETIMES OLDER CHILDREN HAVING TANTRUMS DO regret them and it is so important that they have someone who says, 'It's all right, I can remember doing just the same thing when I was your age,' someone who is on their side rather than someone who tells them off. When I was a young girl often the tiniest thing would set me off shouting and screaming – I used to get terribly angry, real rages of frustration. I remember after one of them my father taking me for a really long walk and never mentioning it – it was wonderful. Walking is excellent for getting things out of your system. Even now if I am not desperately busy but feeling a bit low, I go out and it feels so good to walk and walk. It's a bit like making a fresh start.

They need a hug
When children are little, two-ish or three-ish, they are not embarrassed with themselves or cross about having

had a tantrum, but they may be so relieved when it is over that they hold out their arms for a hug – children sometimes do want to be held and hugged and to feel secure after their tantrum. The storm is over and everything is safe again and they want to be reassured. The tantrum is an explosion of feelings that children can't control and afterwards they do sometimes look as if they wished they hadn't done it, but they can't help it.

Once they get to five or over then they do feel embarrassed and wish they hadn't got so angry and had a tantrum. They mind very much that it has happened and when it's over they get very sad and put their arms around your neck and hug you and have a good old cry. I suppose it's like an adult losing his temper who then regrets it. That's when you should reassure them and not push them away or tell them off.

They don't need a punishment

I have heard people say after the child has had a tantrum in public, 'Right, you're not going to the pantomime,' but you mustn't punish him or expect him to say he's sorry – he couldn't help the tantrum. If you are an adult who is very annoyed you seethe and swear under your breath, but you wouldn't want to be punished for it; rather you want someone to say, 'Let's do something fun to cheer you up.'

I think after a tantrum children do often feel slightly guilty and embarrassed that they have made all this fuss and it hasn't resulted in what they wanted. The sobs tail off and it is terribly sad really, they are so exhausted. A lot of adults find it hard to condone their child's behaviour, but now comes their chance to show their affection to the child, not to criticise or punish, but to reflect to themselves. It is something we all do, it is something I did when I was a child, and so end up cuddling their child instead. The sobs will subside and the thing is not to talk about it any more; you might ask them if they'd like a drink or the child might sniff, 'I'd like a drink of water,' and then it's all over, finished and soon forgotten.

CHAPTER SIX

My Tried and Tested Routines

I USE A ROUTINE RIGHT FROM THE BEGINNING OF THE child's life although I am never rigid about it. It just helps me, and the child, to know where we are – it gives me a structure to work round and it gives the child a knowledge that every day is more or less the same. A child who knows exactly what is going to happen next is a very happy child. Routines are sometimes difficult to continue when you are away from home, but an effort should be made as routine does spell security.

Here are the routines I use on a baby from when he is nine months old. If you would like to know more about my methods of potty training and weaning, there are two more books in this series *Successful Potty Training* and *Easy Weaning and First Feeding* which may be helpful.

Nine Months – One Year Routine

a.m.

7.00 Fruit juice and nappy change then back to bed with a few toys

(This may be earlier or later depending on when your baby wakes up).

8.00 Breakfast, then pot, then play

(Once a baby is nine months I put him on the pot once a day so that he gets used to it. After that I put him in the playpen with a few toys until he can walk at which time I put the playpen away and he plays in the nursery which has a safety gate on the door).

10.00 Put him outside in his pram

(I put him in his pram either sitting-up or lying down or kneeling depending on whether he is a sitter-upper and wrap him up well if it is winter. I give him something to play with and mostly after a while he would just curl up and go to sleep. Very often babies throw the toys out as far as they can and then go to sleep. When he wakes up I don't rush out but leave him there to sit and watch until he has had enough or it is lunchtime. This would be also a good time to take him shopping with you).

p.m.

12.00 Lunch, then nappy change or pot, then play

(From eleven months I would put the baby on the pot

after lunch as well as after breakfast and tea – until then I would change his nappy at this time. As at 8 a.m. I would put him to play in the playpen until he could walk).

2.00 Go to the park

(We would go to the park for two hours unless the weather was bad when we would stay in the nursery. Once we got back I would make tea and he would play in the nursery or come out with me if I had to shop).

4.30 Tea, then pot

(Once the baby was ten months old I put him on the pot after tea as well as after breakfast).

5.00 Play

(This was the time that the children I looked after played with their mother, or in the nursery with building blocks or, once they go older, a game such as Snakes and Ladders).

6.00 Bathtime

6.30 Drink of milk, then bed and story

(Until a baby is nine months old I always feed him last thing at night as I don't think it is fair that he should have his last meal at 6 p.m. Once he is over nine months I would give him a drink of milk now if he asked for it).

One Year To Five Years

For the next four years the routine remains more or less the same. Gradually they will be sitting on the loo rather than having to have their nappy changed, their meals will get larger and they will need less sleep. The main change in routine comes with the introduction of school.

One year old

6.30 p.m. Bed and story.
(At this age I stop giving the baby a drink of milk at bedtime because he has had a mug of milk at tea-time. If a child is thirsty at bedtime then of course I would give him a drink).

Two years old

10 a.m. Go to the park
(I no longer put him out in the pram. Instead I take him to the park for an hour).
11 a.m. Play and juice
(Once we had returned from the park he would play quietly in the nursery for an hour before lunch. On our return from the park I would give him a drink of fruit juice).
12 p.m. Lunch then rest
(After lunch I would put him in his room with a book for roughly an hour, sometimes he fell asleep and

sometimes he didn't. He would be quite happy just to be on his bed. Then he would play in the nursery before we went out to the park again).

Three years old

The routine continues as for the two-year-old unless your child is starting nursery school when it will need some juggling around.

Four years old

11 a.m. Juice and reading lesson
(With a blackboard we would do letters and numbers. I taught all my children to read when they were four).
11.15 a.m. Park
(We would take a ball and meet other children).
1 p.m. Lunch then rest
(No nap was necessary but some children get tired quicker than others. I would put him to bed with a book and sometimes he would just sleep).

A note from Nanny

If your child has the problem of tantrums
you can assure yourself it won't last for ever
– especially not in the form the tantrum is
now. Tantrums do annoy and embarrass
people but with the passing of time a child
becomes an adult and he learns to control
his irritation caused by various situations.

Try always to be on the side of the
child, tantrums or not, and you will then
form a very happy relationship that will
always be there. It is wonderful if a child
can always feel he can rely on you no
matter what problems he may have.

Good luck!

Index